PRAYER JOURNAL for GIRLS

PRAYER CHANGES THINGS

Welcome to your 30-Day Prayer Journal! This journal is a special space just for you - a place to connect with God, reflect on your thoughts, and grow in faith. Each day, you'll find a prompt to guide your prayers and encourage you to think deeply about your relationship with God and the world around you.

Over the next 30 days, you'll explore themes like gratitude, forgiveness, hope, and kindness. These pages are here to help you find peace, understand your purpose, and feel God's presence in your daily life. Write freely, pray with an open heart, and don't be afraid to dream big and seek strength in your faith.

Remember, this journey is yours. There's no right or wrong way to pray or reflect. God listens to every word and knows every thought, so be yourself and trust the process. At the end of these 30 days, you'll be amazed at the growth you've experienced and the closeness you'll feel with God.

Are you ready? Let's begin this journey of faith together.

Today, I am grateful for

____

____

____

____

____

Daily Reminder

Something I'm proud of

____

____

____

____

MY GOALS

Professional Goals

- ○ ______________________
- ○ ______________________
- ○ ______________________
- ○ ______________________
- ○ ______________________

Personal Goals

- ○ ______________________
- ○ ______________________
- ○ ______________________
- ○ ______________________
- ○ ______________________

Health Goals

- ○ ______________________
- ○ ______________________
- ○ ______________________
- ○ ______________________
- ○ ______________________

Financial Goals

- ○ ______________________
- ○ ______________________
- ○ ______________________
- ○ ______________________
- ○ ______________________

Love Goals

- ○ ______________________
- ○ ______________________
- ○ ______________________
- ○ ______________________
- ○ ______________________

Passion Goals

- ○ ______________________
- ○ ______________________
- ○ ______________________
- ○ ______________________
- ○ ______________________

● To Start ☑ Ok → Delay ⊘ Stuck ☒ Cancel

VISION BOARD

(Day): ___________________ (Month): ___________________ (Year): ___________________

REMEMBER
CULTIVATING GRATITUDE IS A POWERFUL PRACTICE THAT CAN POSITIVELY IMPACT YOUR MINDSET AND OVERALL WELL-BEING. ENJOY THIS RITUAL, AND WATCH HOW IT CONTRIBUTES TO A FULFILLED LIFE.

HEALTH

TRAVEL

CAREER

FINANCES

RELATIONSHIPS

SPIRITUALITY

WEEKLY REFLECTIONS

(Day):   (Month):   (Year):

SUMMARIZE KEY EVENT AND ACCOMPLISHMENTS FROM THE WEEK	WHAT WERE YOUR MAJOR ACHIEVEMENTS THIS WEEK?

LIST THREE THINGS YOU'RE GRATEFUL FOR FROM THIS WEEK

IDENTIFY KEY PRIORITIES AND GOALS FOR THE UPCOMING WEEK.

- ○ ________________________________
- ○ ________________________________
- ○ ________________________________
- ○ ________________________________
- ○ ________________________________

● To Start   ☑ Ok   ⊡ Delay   ⊘ Stuck   ⊠ Cancel

Name:_____________________   Date:___________

GRATITUDE JAR

In the jar below, please write down everything you are thankful for!

Name:____________________   Date:____________

# REFLECTIONS JAR

In the jar below, please write down everything you are thankful for!

Name:____________________   Date:___________

GOODNESS JAR

In the jar below, please write down everything you are thankful for!

On every good deed or a job done you will get a star

Name:_____________________   Date:___________

SAVING JAR

In the jar below, please write down everything you are thankful for!

On every saving you will
get a heart

90 heart

Saving Place : _______________

Start Date : _________________

Goal :

SELF REFLECTION

IM GRATEFUL FOR ...

APPRECIATION

THINGS I AM VERY GOOD AT ...

DREAM JOURNAL

(Remember)

EMBARK ON A SACRED JOURNEY WITHIN THROUGH DAILY DREAM JOURNALING—A SPIRITUAL PRACTICE THAT UPLIFTS YOUR MINDSET AND NURTURES WELL-BEING.

(Day):   (Month):   (Year):

(DreamOverview)   RECORD A DETAILED DESCRIPTION OF THE DREAM. INCLUDE PEOPLE, PLACES, EMOTIONS, AND ANY VIVID DETAILS.

Mood Tracker	○ ○ ○ ○ ○		(People and Relationships)
Lucidity Level	○ ○ ○ ○ ○		
Sleep Quality	○ ○ ○ ○ ○		
Recurring?	YES ○ NO ○		
Interrupted?	YES ○ NO ○		

(Emotions Felt)   NOTE THE EMOTIONS EXPERIENCED DURING THE DREAM. HOW DID THE DREAM MAKE YOU FEEL

(Interpretation)   DIVE DEEP INTO DREAM INTERPRETATION—DECODE MESSAGES, SYMBOLS, AND INSIGHT

PLAN FOR THE DAY

PRIORITIES

TODAY'S MOOD:   

MEAL TRACKER

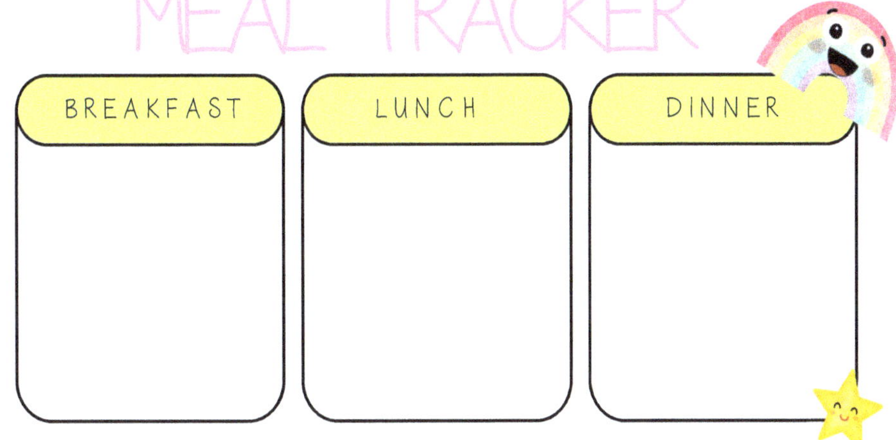

BREAKFAST	LUNCH	DINNER

MY PRAYER JOURNAL

DATE: /   /

HOW ARE YOU FEELING?
(CIRCLE YOUR MOOD)

EXCITED HAPPY CHILL GRATEFUL

ANGRY WORRIED FRUSTRATED SAD

TODAY, I AM GRATEFUL FOR...

1 ___________________________

2 ___________________________

3 ___________________________

I AM SORRY FOR...

MEMORY VERSE

WHO CAN I PRAY FOR TODAY?

TODAY, I AM PRAYING FOR...

LETTERS TO GOD

DEAR GOD,

LOVE,

LETTERS TO GOD

DEAR GOD,

LOVE,

MY PRAYER JOURNAL

DATE: / /

HOW ARE YOU FEELING?
(CIRCLE YOUR MOOD)

EXCITED HAPPY CHILL GRATEFUL

ANGRY WORRIED FRUSTRATED SAD

TODAY, I AM GRATEFUL FOR...

1 ....

2 ....

3 ....

I AM SORRY FOR...

....

....

....

....

MEMORY VERSE

....

....

....

....

....

....

....

WHO CAN I PRAY FOR TODAY?

TODAY, I AM PRAYING FOR...

....

....

....

....

....

LETTERS TO GOD
DEAR GOD,
LOVE,

LETTERS TO GOD
DEAR GOD,
LOVE,

MY PRAYER JOURNAL

DATE: /   /

HOW ARE YOU FEELING?
(CIRCLE YOUR MOOD)

EXCITED   HAPPY   CHILL   GRATEFUL

ANGRY   WORRIED   FRUSTRATED   SAD

TODAY, I AM GRATEFUL FOR...

1 ....

2 ....

3 ....

I AM SORRY FOR...

MEMORY VERSE

WHO CAN I PRAY FOR TODAY?

TODAY, I AM PRAYING FOR...

LETTERS TO GOD

DEAR GOD,

LOVE,

LETTERS TO GOD

DEAR GOD,

LOVE,

MY PRAYER JOURNAL

DATE: /   /

HOW ARE YOU FEELING?
(CIRCLE YOUR MOOD)

EXCITED HAPPY CHILL GRATEFUL

ANGRY WORRIED FRUSTRATED SAD

TODAY, I AM GRATEFUL FOR...

1 ____________________________

2 ____________________________

3 ____________________________

I AM SORRY FOR...

____

____

____

____

MEMORY VERSE

____

____

____

____

____

____

____

WHO CAN I PRAY FOR TODAY?

TODAY, I AM PRAYING FOR...

____

____

____

____

LETTERS TO GOD

DEAR GOD,

LOVE,

LETTERS TO GOD

DEAR GOD,

LOVE,

DATE: /   /

HOW ARE YOU FEELING?
(CIRCLE YOUR MOOD)

EXCITED   HAPPY   CHILL   GRATEFUL

ANGRY   WORRIED   FRUSTRATED   SAD

TODAY, I AM GRATEFUL FOR...

1
2
3

I AM SORRY FOR...

MEMORY VERSE

WHO CAN I PRAY FOR TODAY?

TODAY, I AM PRAYING FOR...

LETTERS TO GOD

DEAR GOD,

LOVE,

LETTERS TO GOD

DEAR GOD,

LOVE,

MY PRAYER JOURNAL

DATE: / /

HOW ARE YOU FEELING?
(CIRCLE YOUR MOOD)

EXCITED   HAPPY   CHILL   GRATEFUL

ANGRY   WORRIED   FRUSTRATED   SAD

TODAY, I AM GRATEFUL FOR...

1

2

3

I AM SORRY FOR...

MEMORY VERSE

WHO CAN I PRAY FOR TODAY?

TODAY, I AM PRAYING FOR...

LETTERS TO GOD

DEAR GOD,

LOVE,

LETTERS TO GOD

DEAR GOD,

LOVE,

MY PRAYER JOURNAL

DATE: / /

HOW ARE YOU FEELING?
(CIRCLE YOUR MOOD)

EXCITED HAPPY CHILL GRATEFUL

ANGRY WORRIED FRUSTRATED SAD

TODAY, I AM GRATEFUL FOR...

1
2
3

I AM SORRY FOR...

MEMORY VERSE

WHO CAN I PRAY FOR TODAY?

TODAY, I AM PRAYING FOR...

LETTERS TO GOD

DEAR GOD,

LOVE,

LETTERS TO GOD

DEAR GOD,

LOVE,

MY PRAYER JOURNAL

DATE: / /

HOW ARE YOU FEELING?
(CIRCLE YOUR MOOD)

EXCITED HAPPY CHILL GRATEFUL

ANGRY WORRIED FRUSTRATED SAD

TODAY, I AM GRATEFUL FOR...

1 ______________________________

2 ______________________________

3 ______________________________

I AM SORRY FOR...

MEMORY VERSE

WHO CAN I PRAY FOR TODAY?

TODAY, I AM PRAYING FOR...

LETTERS TO GOD

DEAR GOD,

LOVE,

LETTERS TO GOD

DEAR GOD,

LOVE,

MY PRAYER JOURNAL

DATE: / /

HOW ARE YOU FEELING?
(CIRCLE YOUR MOOD)

EXCITED   HAPPY   CHILL   GRATEFUL

ANGRY   WORRIED   FRUSTRATED   SAD

TODAY, I AM GRATEFUL FOR...

1 ....

2 ....

3 ....

I AM SORRY FOR...

MEMORY VERSE

WHO CAN I PRAY FOR TODAY?

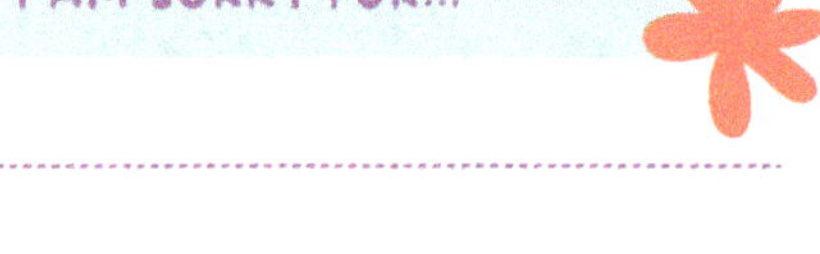

TODAY, I AM PRAYING FOR...

LETTERS TO GOD

DEAR GOD,

LOVE,

LETTERS TO GOD

DEAR GOD,

LOVE,

DATE: / /

HOW ARE YOU FEELING?
(CIRCLE YOUR MOOD)

EXCITED   HAPPY   CHILL   GRATEFUL

ANGRY   WORRIED   FRUSTRATED   SAD

TODAY, I AM GRATEFUL FOR...

1 ....

2 ....

3 ....

I AM SORRY FOR...

....

....

....

....

MEMORY VERSE

....

....

....

....

....

....

....

WHO CAN I PRAY FOR TODAY?

TODAY, I AM PRAYING FOR...

....

....

....

....

LETTERS TO GOD

DEAR GOD,

LOVE,

LETTERS TO GOD

DEAR GOD,

LOVE,

DATE: /   /

HOW ARE YOU FEELING?
(CIRCLE YOUR MOOD)

EXCITED   HAPPY   CHILL   GRATEFUL

ANGRY   WORRIED   FRUSTRATED   SAD

TODAY, I AM GRATEFUL FOR...

1 ______________________________

2 ______________________________

3 ______________________________

I AM SORRY FOR...

____

____

____

____

MEMORY VERSE

____

____

____

____

____

____

____

WHO CAN I PRAY FOR TODAY?

TODAY, I AM PRAYING FOR...

____

____

____

____

____

LETTERS TO GOD
DEAR GOD,
LOVE,

LETTERS TO GOD
DEAR GOD,
LOVE,

MY PRAYER JOURNAL

DATE: / /

HOW ARE YOU FEELING?
(CIRCLE YOUR MOOD)

EXCITED   HAPPY   CHILL   GRATEFUL

ANGRY   WORRIED   FRUSTRATED   SAD

TODAY, I AM GRATEFUL FOR...

1 ....

2 ....

3 ....

I AM SORRY FOR...

....

....

....

....

MEMORY VERSE

....
....
....
....
....
....
....

WHO CAN I PRAY FOR TODAY?

TODAY, I AM PRAYING FOR...

....

....

....

....

LETTERS TO GOD
DEAR GOD,
LOVE,

LETTERS TO GOD
DEAR GOD,
LOVE,

MY PRAYER JOURNAL

DATE: /   /

HOW ARE YOU FEELING?
(CIRCLE YOUR MOOD)

EXCITED   HAPPY   CHILL   GRATEFUL

ANGRY   WORRIED   FRUSTRATED   SAD

TODAY, I AM GRATEFUL FOR...

1 ....

2 ....

3 ....

I AM SORRY FOR...

....

....

....

....

MEMORY VERSE

....

....

....

....

....

....

....

WHO CAN I PRAY FOR TODAY?

TODAY, I AM PRAYING FOR...

....

....

....

....

LETTERS TO GOD

DEAR GOD,

LOVE,

LETTERS TO GOD

DEAR GOD,

LOVE,

MY PRAYER JOURNAL

DATE: /   /

HOW ARE YOU FEELING?
(CIRCLE YOUR MOOD)

EXCITED   HAPPY   CHILL   GRATEFUL

ANGRY   WORRIED   FRUSTRATED   SAD

TODAY, I AM GRATEFUL FOR...

1
2
3

I AM SORRY FOR...

MEMORY VERSE

WHO CAN I PRAY FOR TODAY?

TODAY, I AM PRAYING FOR...

LETTERS TO GOD

DEAR GOD,

LOVE,

LETTERS TO GOD

DEAR GOD,

LOVE,

MY PRAYER JOURNAL

DATE: /   /

HOW ARE YOU FEELING?
(CIRCLE YOUR MOOD)

EXCITED   HAPPY   CHILL   GRATEFUL

ANGRY   WORRIED   FRUSTRATED   SAD

TODAY, I AM GRATEFUL FOR...

1 ____________________

2 ____________________

3 ____________________

I AM SORRY FOR...

____

____

____

____

MEMORY VERSE

WHO CAN I PRAY FOR TODAY?

TODAY, I AM PRAYING FOR...

LETTERS TO GOD

DEAR GOD,

LOVE,

LETTERS TO GOD

DEAR GOD,

LOVE,

MY PRAYER JOURNAL

DATE: /   /

HOW ARE YOU FEELING?
(CIRCLE YOUR MOOD)

EXCITED HAPPY CHILL GRATEFUL

ANGRY WORRIED FRUSTRATED SAD

TODAY, I AM GRATEFUL FOR...

1 ....

2 ....

3 ....

I AM SORRY FOR...

....

....

....

....

MEMORY VERSE

....

....

....

....

....

....

....

WHO CAN I PRAY FOR TODAY?

TODAY, I AM PRAYING FOR...

....

....

....

....

LETTERS TO GOD

DEAR GOD,

LOVE,

LETTERS TO GOD

DEAR GOD,

LOVE,

DATE: / /

HOW ARE YOU FEELING?
(CIRCLE YOUR MOOD)

EXCITED   HAPPY   CHILL   GRATEFUL

ANGRY   WORRIED   FRUSTRATED   SAD

TODAY, I AM GRATEFUL FOR...

1 ______________________________

2 ______________________________

3 ______________________________

I AM SORRY FOR...

____
____
____
____

MEMORY VERSE

WHO CAN I PRAY FOR TODAY?

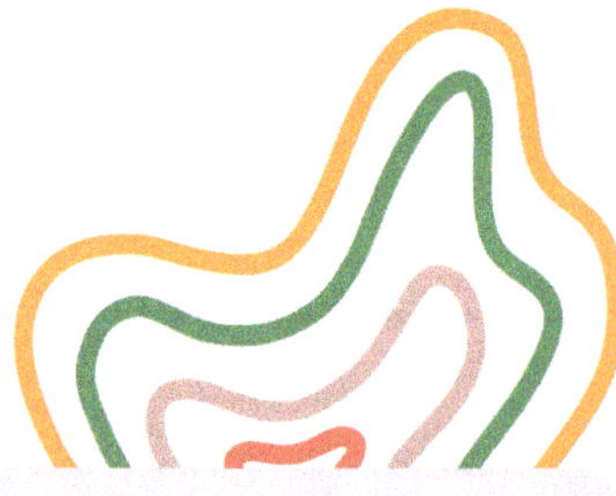

TODAY, I AM PRAYING FOR...

____
____
____
____

LETTERS TO GOD

DEAR GOD,

LOVE,

LETTERS TO GOD

DEAR GOD,

LOVE,

MY PRAYER JOURNAL

DATE: / /

HOW ARE YOU FEELING?
(CIRCLE YOUR MOOD)

EXCITED   HAPPY   CHILL   GRATEFUL

ANGRY   WORRIED   FRUSTRATED   SAD

TODAY, I AM GRATEFUL FOR...

1 ....

2 ....

3 ....

I AM SORRY FOR...

MEMORY VERSE

WHO CAN I PRAY FOR TODAY?

TODAY, I AM PRAYING FOR...

LETTERS TO GOD

DEAR GOD,

LOVE,

LETTERS TO GOD

DEAR GOD,

LOVE,

MY PRAYER JOURNAL

DATE: / /

HOW ARE YOU FEELING?
(CIRCLE YOUR MOOD)

EXCITED   HAPPY   CHILL   GRATEFUL

ANGRY   WORRIED   FRUSTRATED   SAD

TODAY, I AM GRATEFUL FOR...

1 ....
2 ....
3 ....

I AM SORRY FOR...

....
....
....
....

MEMORY VERSE

....
....
....
....
....
....
....

WHO CAN I PRAY FOR TODAY?

TODAY, I AM PRAYING FOR...

....
....
....
....
....

LETTERS TO GOD
DEAR GOD,
LOVE,

LETTERS TO GOD
DEAR GOD,
LOVE,

MY PRAYER JOURNAL

DATE: / /

HOW ARE YOU FEELING?
(CIRCLE YOUR MOOD)

EXCITED   HAPPY   CHILL   GRATEFUL

ANGRY   WORRIED   FRUSTRATED   SAD

TODAY, I AM GRATEFUL FOR...

1 ______________________________

2 ______________________________

3 ______________________________

I AM SORRY FOR...

____

____

____

____

MEMORY VERSE

____

____

____

____

____

____

____

WHO CAN I PRAY FOR TODAY?

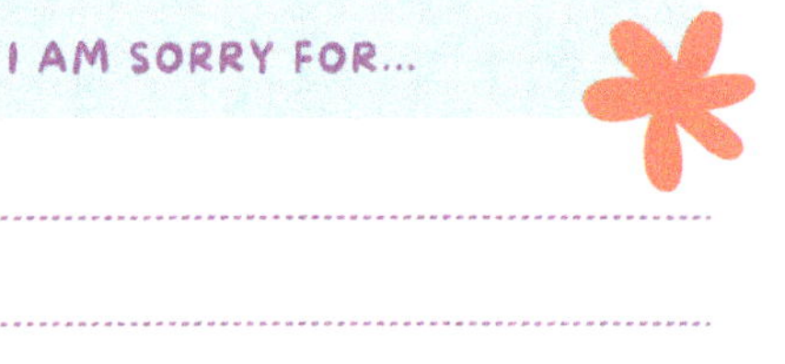

TODAY, I AM PRAYING FOR...

____

____

____

____

____

LETTERS TO GOD

DEAR GOD,

LOVE,

LETTERS TO GOD

DEAR GOD,

LOVE,

MY PRAYER JOURNAL

DATE: /   /

HOW ARE YOU FEELING?
(CIRCLE YOUR MOOD)

EXCITED   HAPPY   CHILL   GRATEFUL

ANGRY   WORRIED   FRUSTRATED   SAD

TODAY, I AM GRATEFUL FOR...

1 ....
2 ....
3 ....

I AM SORRY FOR...

....
....
....
....

MEMORY VERSE

....
....
....
....
....
....
....

WHO CAN I PRAY FOR TODAY?

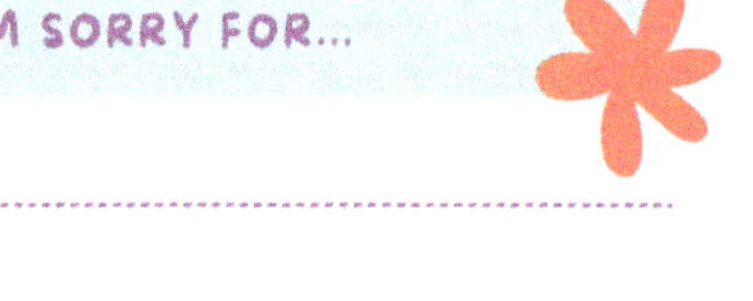

TODAY, I AM PRAYING FOR...

....
....
....
....
....

LETTERS TO GOD

DEAR GOD,

LOVE,

LETTERS TO GOD

DEAR GOD,

LOVE,

MY PRAYER JOURNAL

DATE: / /

HOW ARE YOU FEELING?
(CIRCLE YOUR MOOD)

EXCITED HAPPY CHILL GRATEFUL

ANGRY WORRIED FRUSTRATED SAD

TODAY, I AM GRATEFUL FOR...

1 ------------------------------------

2 ------------------------------------

3 ------------------------------------

I AM SORRY FOR...

MEMORY VERSE

WHO CAN I PRAY FOR TODAY?

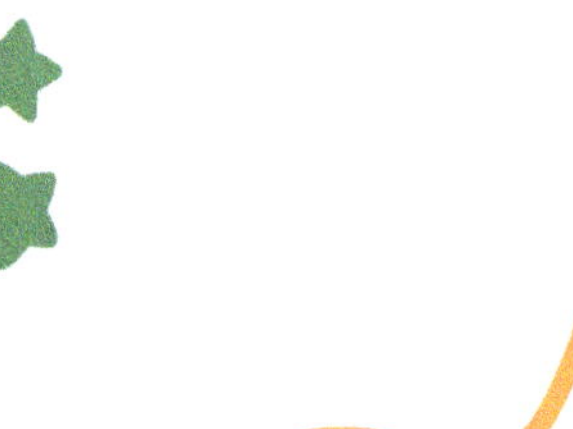

TODAY, I AM PRAYING FOR...

LETTERS TO GOD

DEAR GOD,

LOVE,

LETTERS TO GOD

DEAR GOD,

LOVE,

DATE: /   /

HOW ARE YOU FEELING?
(CIRCLE YOUR MOOD)

EXCITED   HAPPY   CHILL   GRATEFUL

ANGRY   WORRIED   FRUSTRATED   SAD

TODAY, I AM GRATEFUL FOR...

1 __________________________________

2 __________________________________

3 __________________________________

I AM SORRY FOR...

____

____

____

____

MEMORY VERSE

____
____
____
____
____
____
____

WHO CAN I PRAY FOR TODAY?

TODAY, I AM PRAYING FOR...

____
____
____
____
____

LETTERS TO GOD
DEAR GOD,
LOVE,

LETTERS TO GOD
DEAR GOD,
LOVE,

MY PRAYER JOURNAL

DATE: / /

HOW ARE YOU FEELING?
(CIRCLE YOUR MOOD)

EXCITED   HAPPY   CHILL   GRATEFUL

ANGRY   WORRIED   FRUSTRATED   SAD

TODAY, I AM GRATEFUL FOR...

1 ....

2 ....

3 ....

I AM SORRY FOR...

....

....

....

....

MEMORY VERSE

....

....

....

....

....

....

....

WHO CAN I PRAY FOR TODAY?

TODAY, I AM PRAYING FOR...

....

....

....

....

LETTERS TO GOD

DEAR GOD,

LOVE,

LETTERS TO GOD

DEAR GOD,

LOVE,

MY PRAYER JOURNAL

DATE: /   /

HOW ARE YOU FEELING?
(CIRCLE YOUR MOOD)

EXCITED   HAPPY   CHILL   GRATEFUL

ANGRY   WORRIED   FRUSTRATED   SAD

TODAY, I AM GRATEFUL FOR...

1
2
3

I AM SORRY FOR...

MEMORY VERSE

WHO CAN I PRAY FOR TODAY?

TODAY, I AM PRAYING FOR...

LETTERS TO GOD

DEAR GOD,

LOVE,

LETTERS TO GOD

DEAR GOD,

LOVE,

MY PRAYER JOURNAL

DATE: /   /

HOW ARE YOU FEELING?
(CIRCLE YOUR MOOD)

EXCITED   HAPPY   CHILL   GRATEFUL

ANGRY   WORRIED   FRUSTRATED   SAD

TODAY, I AM GRATEFUL FOR...

1 ____________________

2 ____________________

3 ____________________

I AM SORRY FOR...

MEMORY VERSE

WHO CAN I PRAY FOR TODAY?

TODAY, I AM PRAYING FOR...

LETTERS TO GOD
DEAR GOD,
LOVE,

LETTERS TO GOD
DEAR GOD,
LOVE,

MY PRAYER JOURNAL

DATE: / /

HOW ARE YOU FEELING?
(CIRCLE YOUR MOOD)

EXCITED HAPPY CHILL GRATEFUL

ANGRY WORRIED FRUSTRATED SAD

TODAY, I AM GRATEFUL FOR...

1 ....

2 ....

3 ....

I AM SORRY FOR...

....

....

....

....

MEMORY VERSE

....

....

....

....

....

....

....

WHO CAN I PRAY FOR TODAY?

TODAY, I AM PRAYING FOR...

....

....

....

....

LETTERS TO GOD

DEAR GOD,

LOVE,

LETTERS TO GOD

DEAR GOD,

LOVE,

MY PRAYER JOURNAL

DATE: /   /

HOW ARE YOU FEELING?
(CIRCLE YOUR MOOD)

EXCITED   HAPPY   CHILL   GRATEFUL

ANGRY   WORRIED   FRUSTRATED   SAD

TODAY, I AM GRATEFUL FOR...

1

2

3

I AM SORRY FOR...

MEMORY VERSE

WHO CAN I PRAY FOR TODAY?

TODAY, I AM PRAYING FOR...

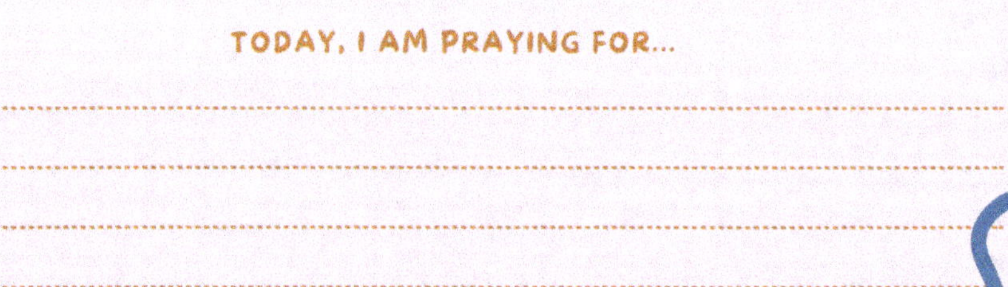

LETTERS TO GOD

DEAR GOD,

LOVE,

LETTERS TO GOD

DEAR GOD,

LOVE,

MY PRAYER JOURNAL

DATE: / /

HOW ARE YOU FEELING?
(CIRCLE YOUR MOOD)

EXCITED HAPPY CHILL GRATEFUL

ANGRY WORRIED FRUSTRATED SAD

TODAY, I AM GRATEFUL FOR...

1 ______________________________

2 ______________________________

3 ______________________________

I AM SORRY FOR...

____

____

____

____

MEMORY VERSE

____

____

____

____

____

____

____

WHO CAN I PRAY FOR TODAY?

TODAY, I AM PRAYING FOR...

____

____

____

____

____

LETTERS TO GOD

DEAR GOD,

LOVE,

LETTERS TO GOD

DEAR GOD,

LOVE,

MY PRAYER JOURNAL

DATE: /   /

HOW ARE YOU FEELING?
(CIRCLE YOUR MOOD)

EXCITED HAPPY CHILL GRATEFUL

ANGRY WORRIED FRUSTRATED SAD

TODAY, I AM GRATEFUL FOR...

1 ....

2 ....

3 ....

I AM SORRY FOR...

....

....

....

....

MEMORY VERSE

....

....

....

....

....

....

WHO CAN I PRAY FOR TODAY?

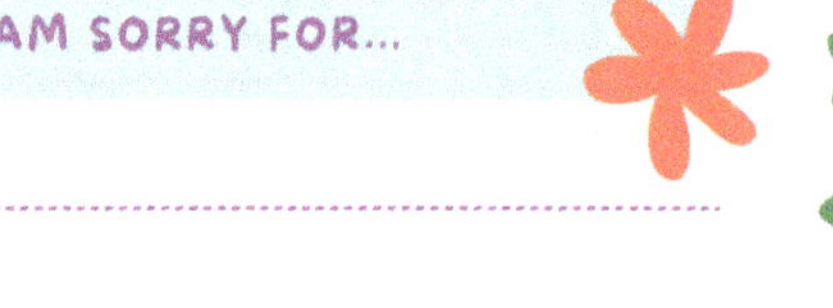

TODAY, I AM PRAYING FOR...

....

....

....

....

....

LETTERS TO GOD

DEAR GOD,

LOVE,

LETTERS TO GOD

DEAR GOD,

LOVE,

JOURNAL

JOURNAL

JOURNAL

Congratulations on completing your 30-day journey in this prayer journal! You've taken time each day to connect with God, reflect on your thoughts, and strengthen your faith. This is something truly special, and you should be proud of the commitment you've made to nurture your spiritual growth.

As you move forward, remember that prayer and reflection don't end here. You can continue to use what you've learned and felt in these pages as a foundation for your ongoing journey with God. Whenever you feel joy, gratitude, worry, or need guidance, know that you can turn to Him at any time, just like you've done each day in this journal.

Thank you for being part of this beautiful journey. May you carry forward the peace, love, and strength you've found here. Remember that God is always with you, cheering you on and guiding you through every step of your life.

Blessings and love on all the adventures ahead!